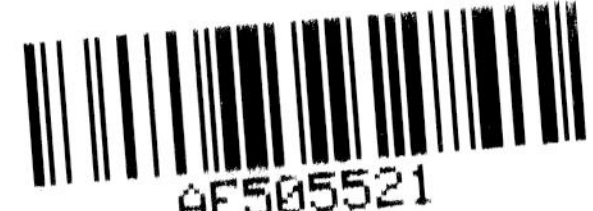

MILITAIRE
Livre de coloriage

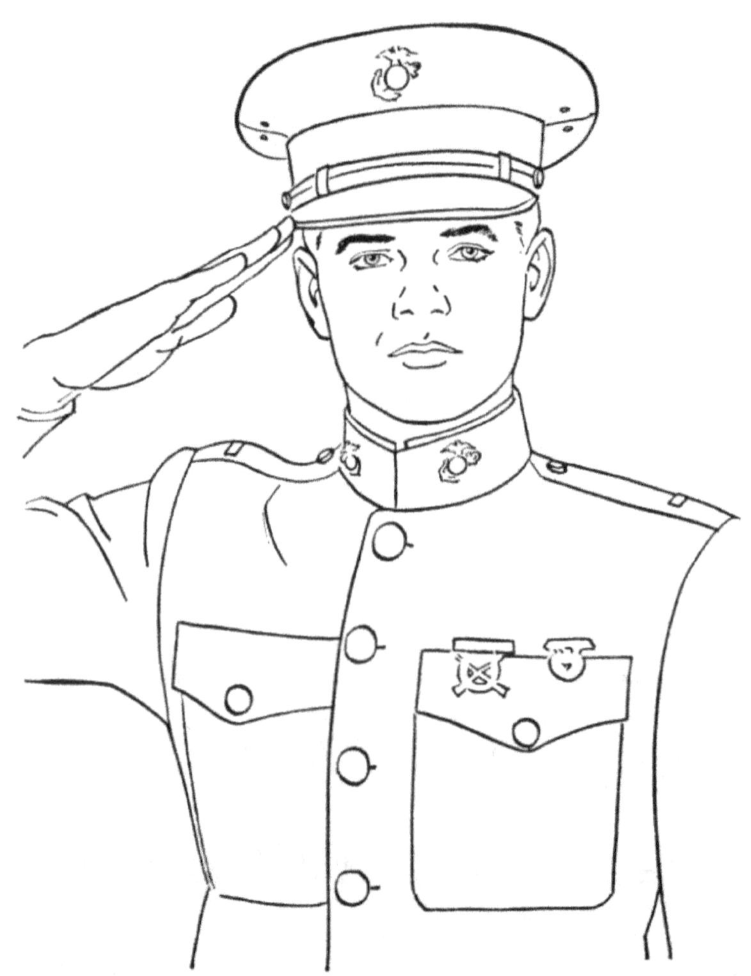

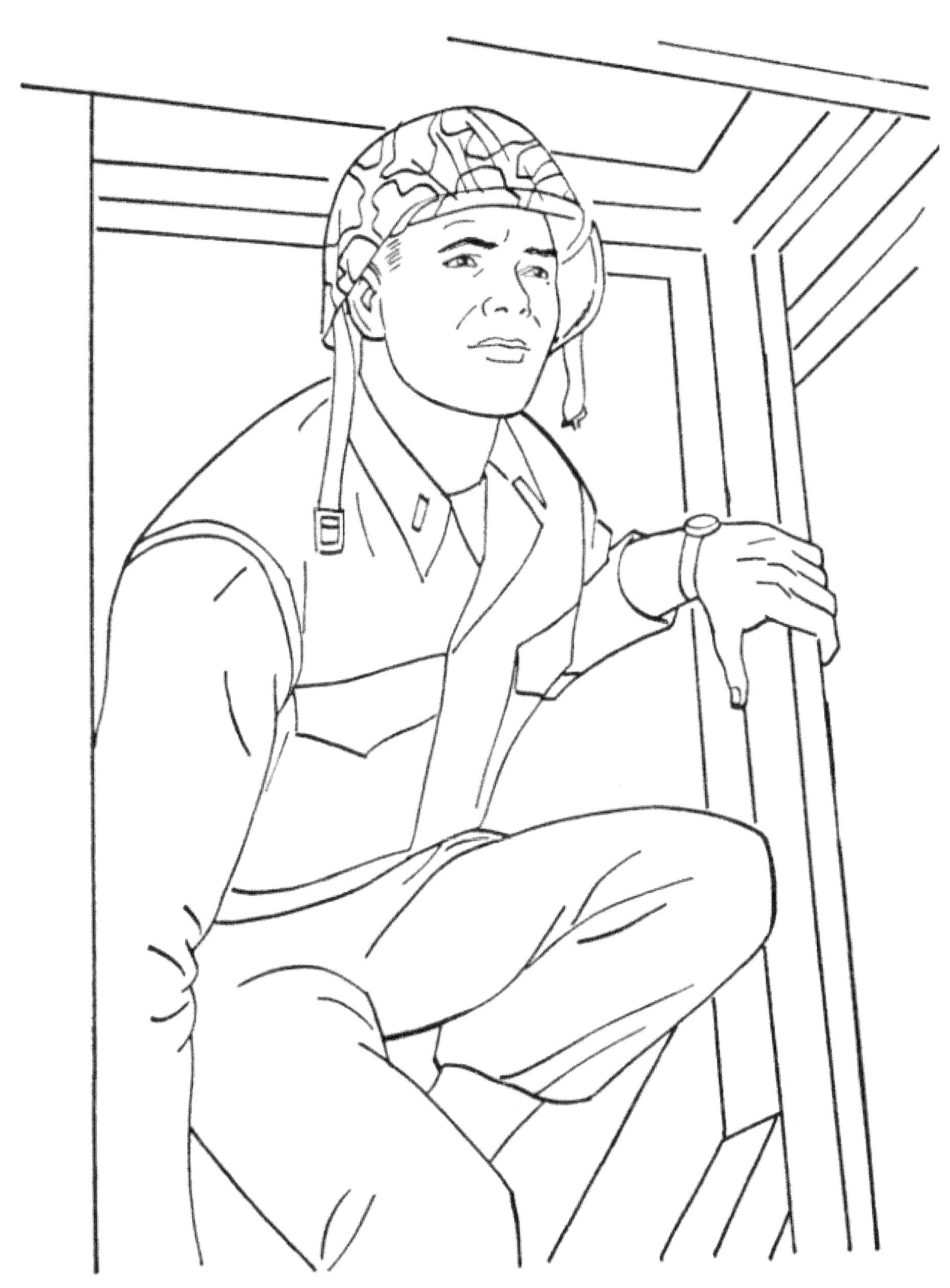

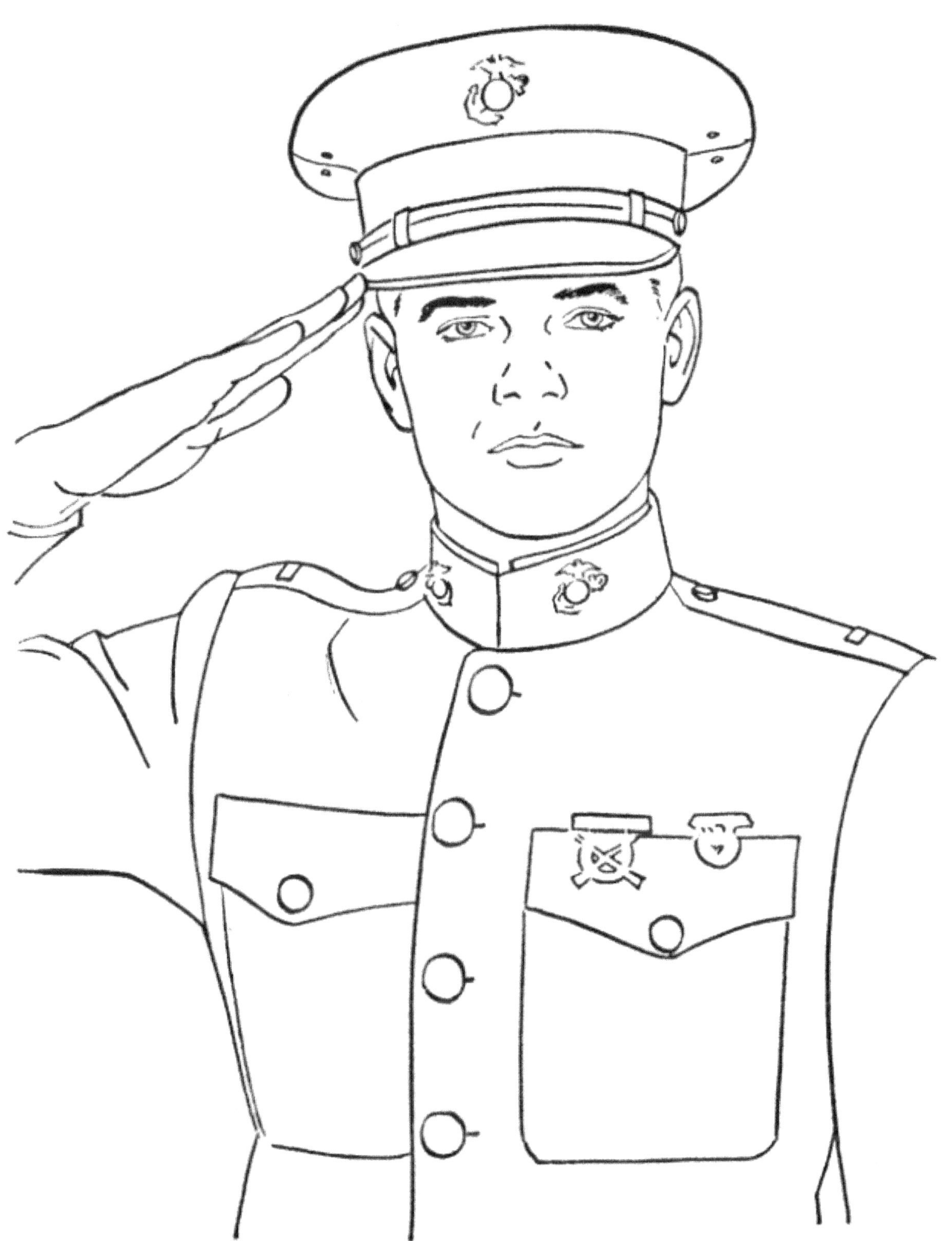

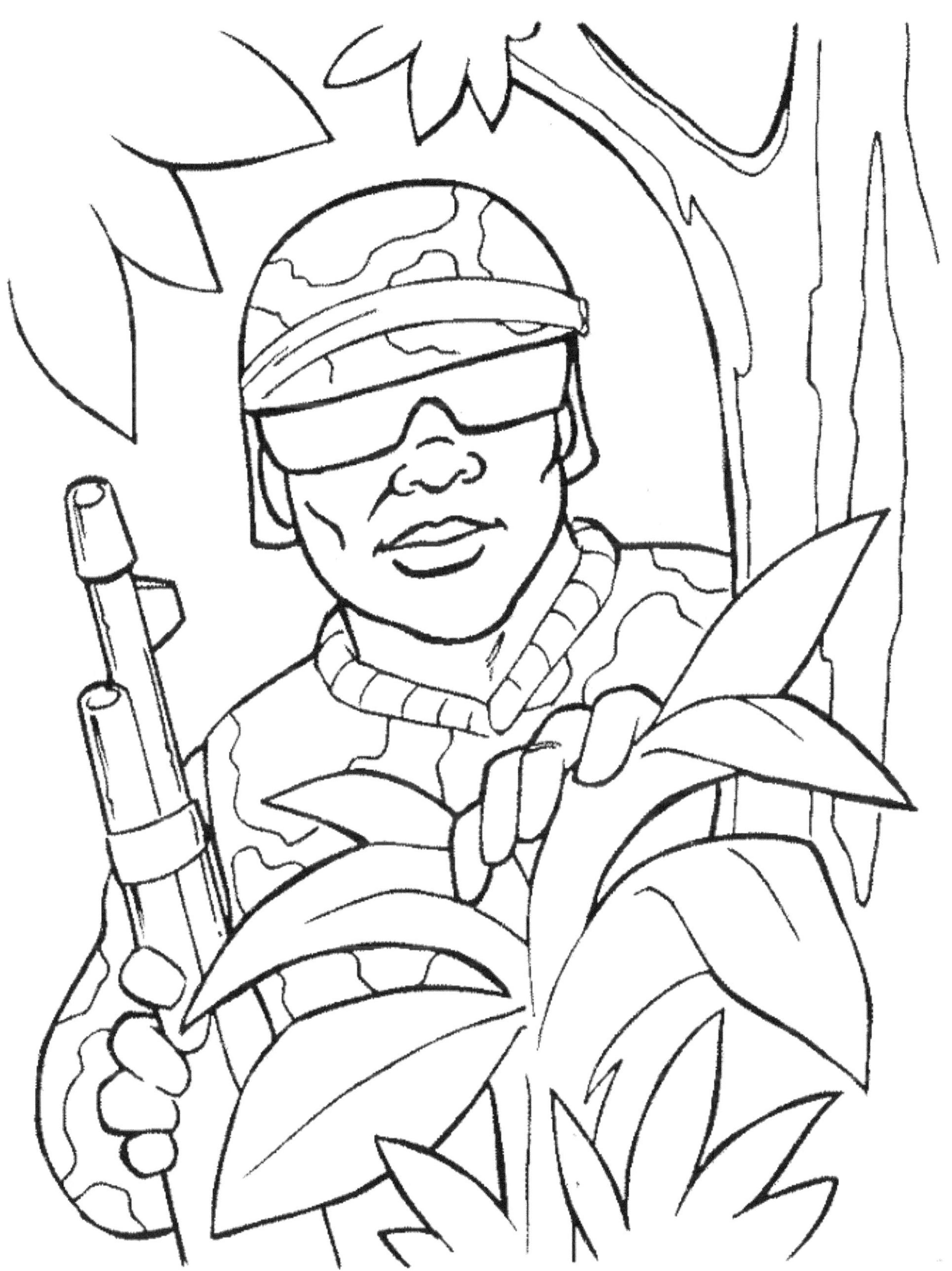

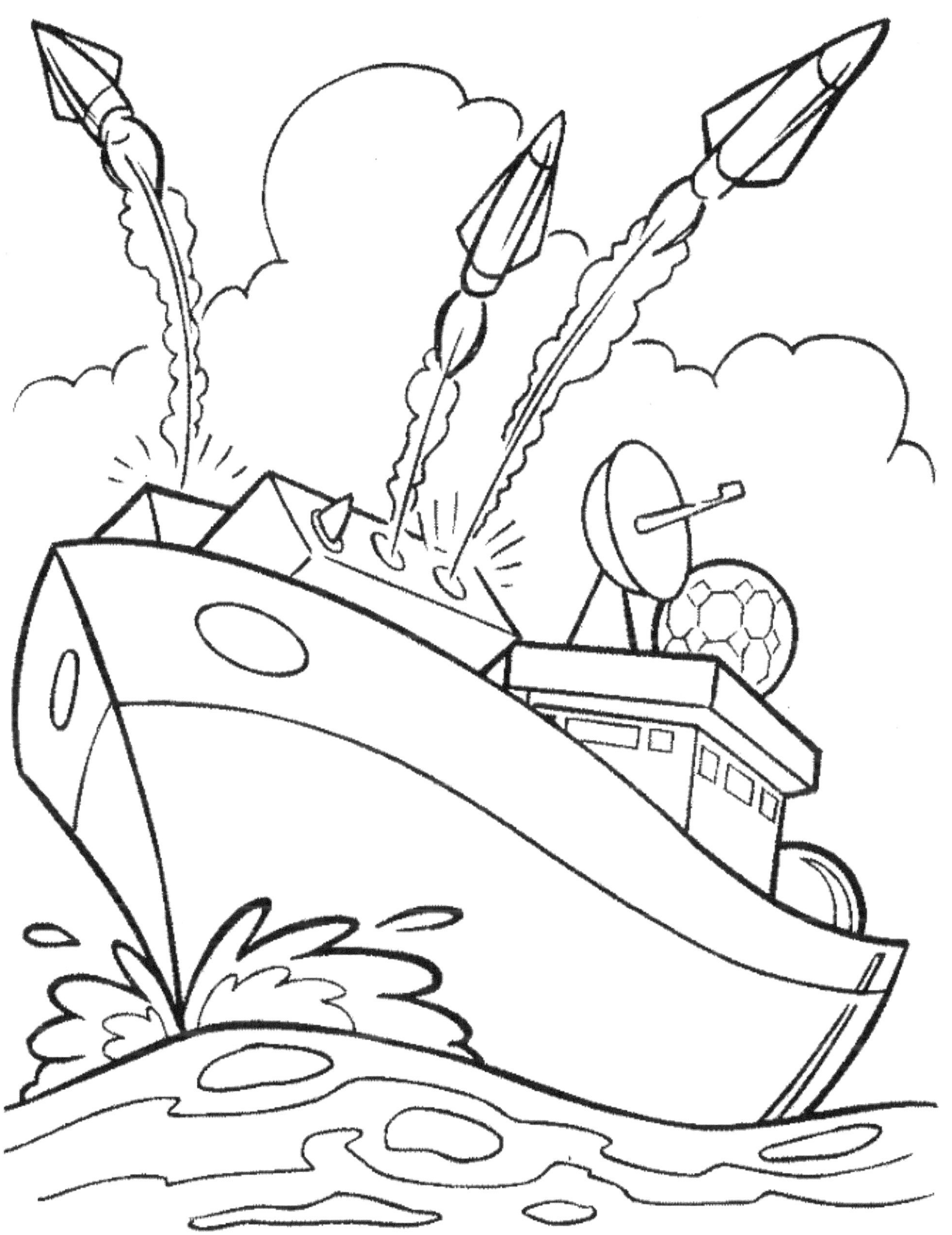

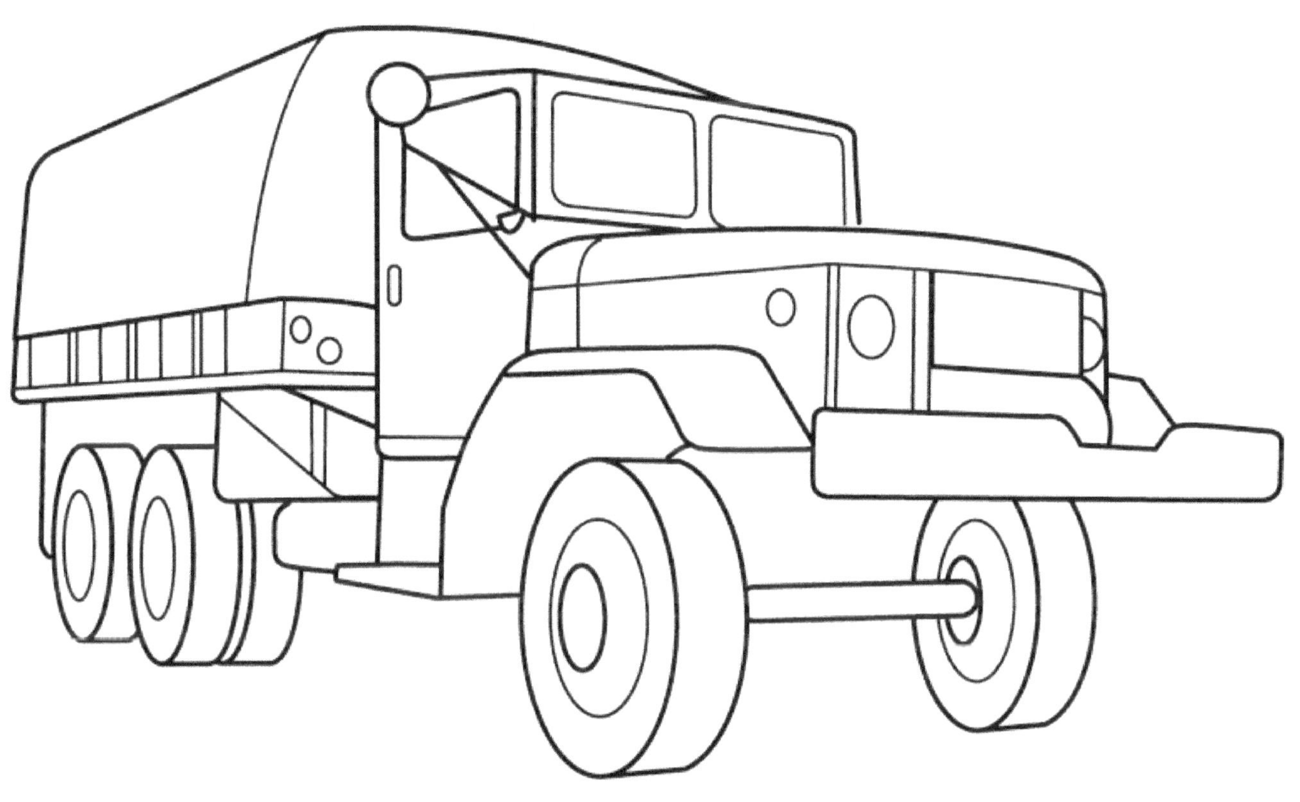

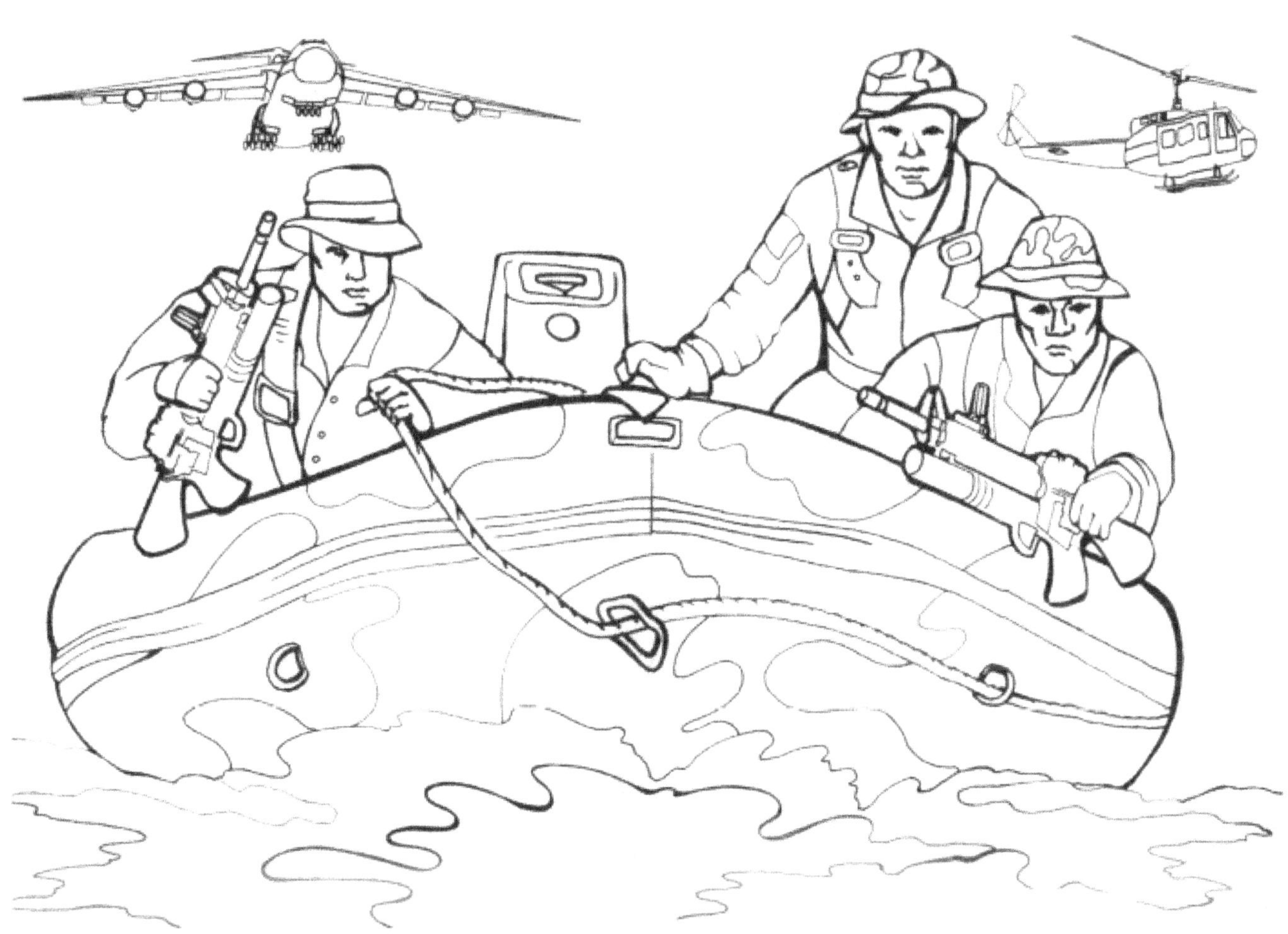

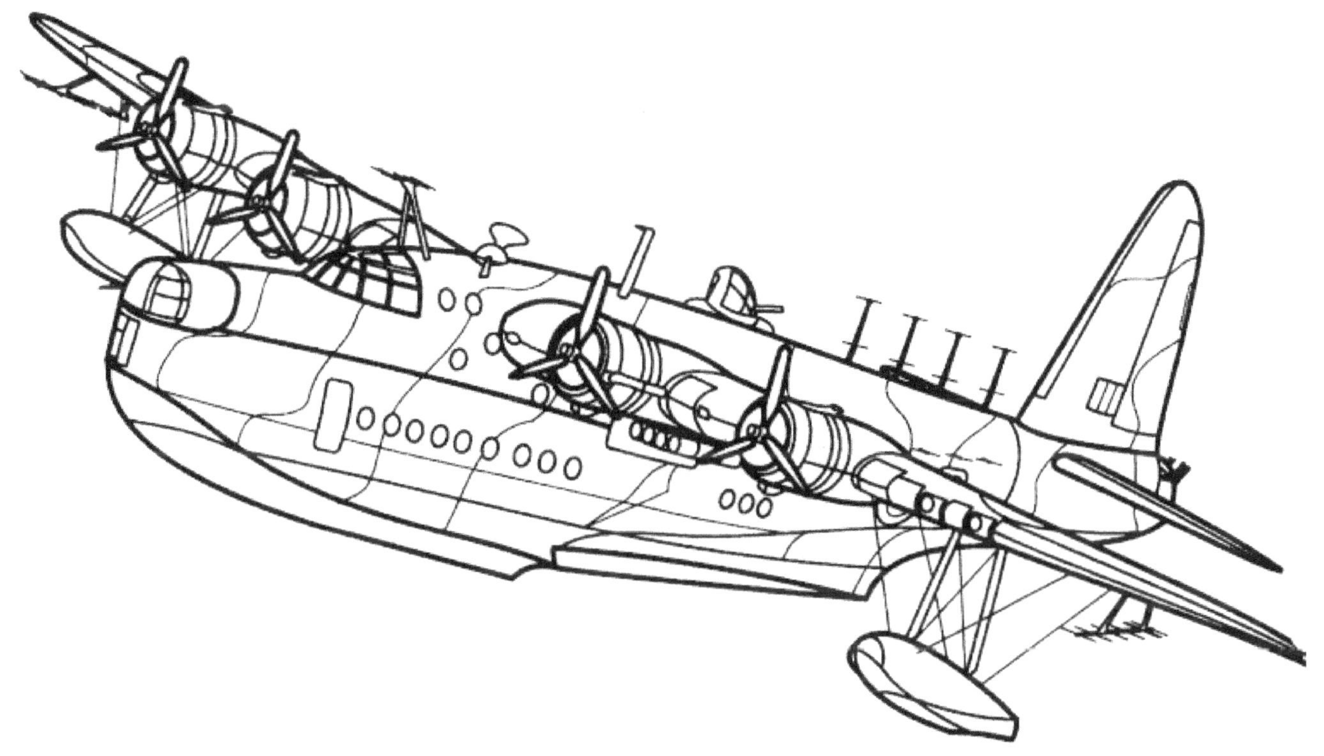

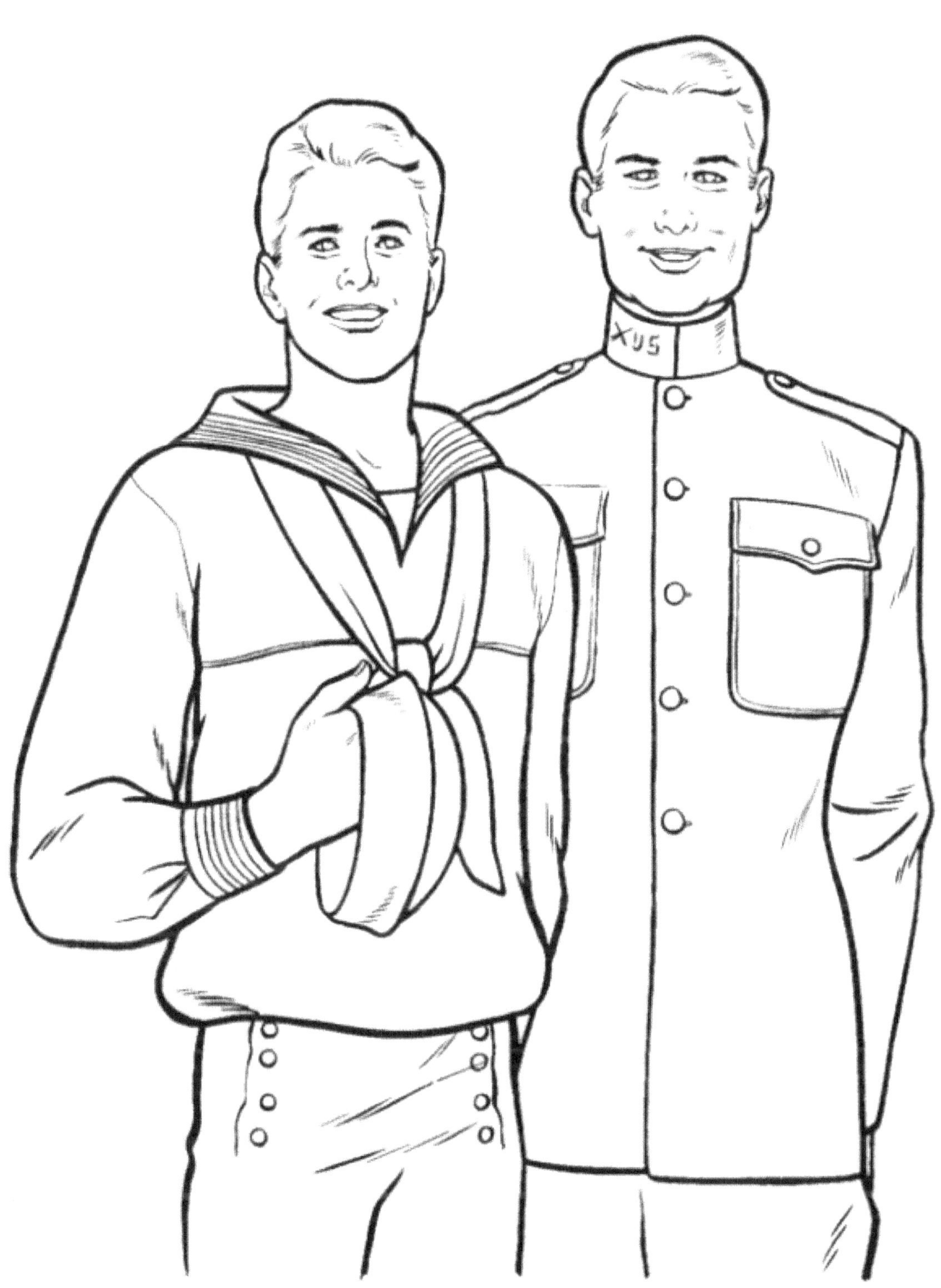
XUS

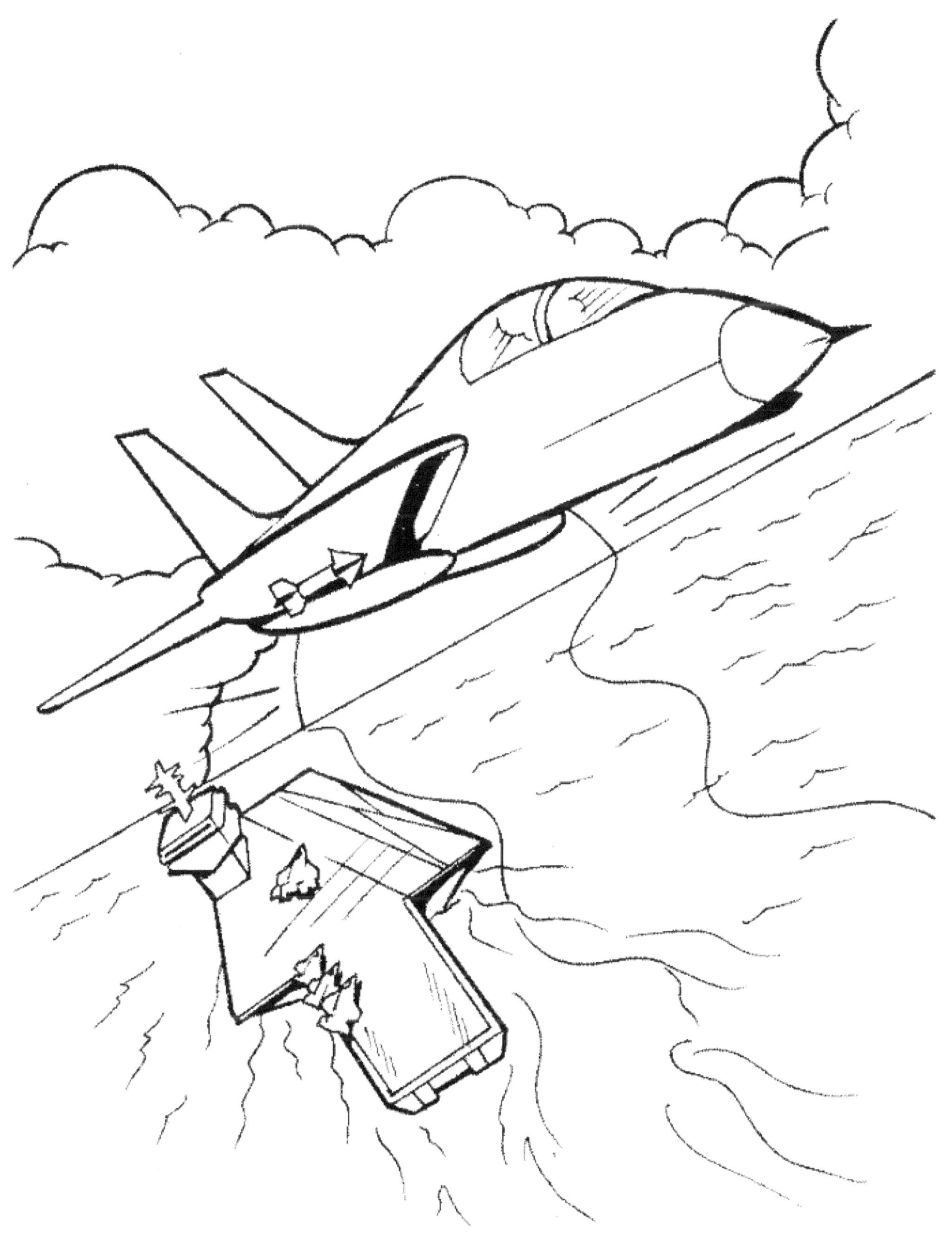

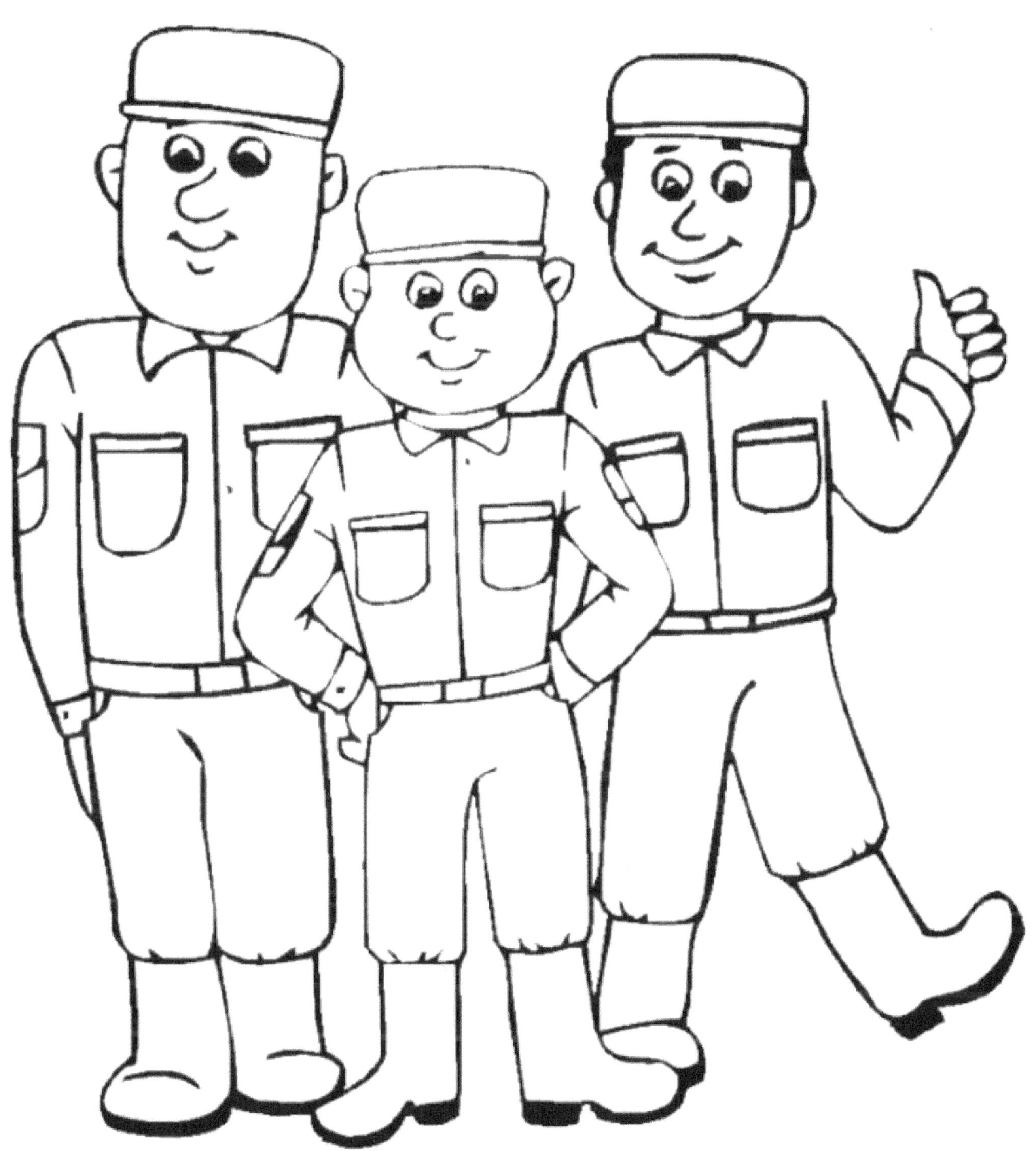

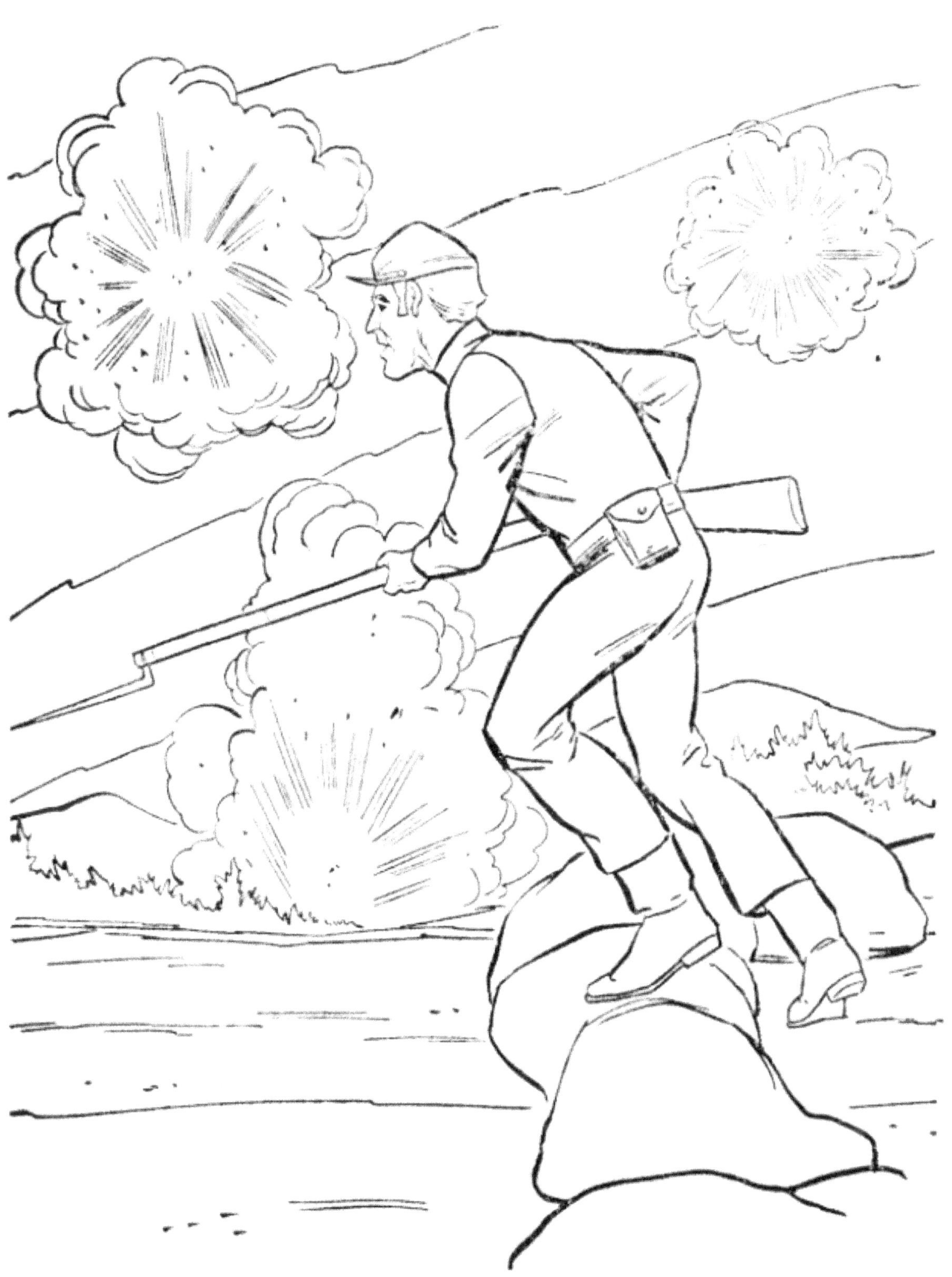

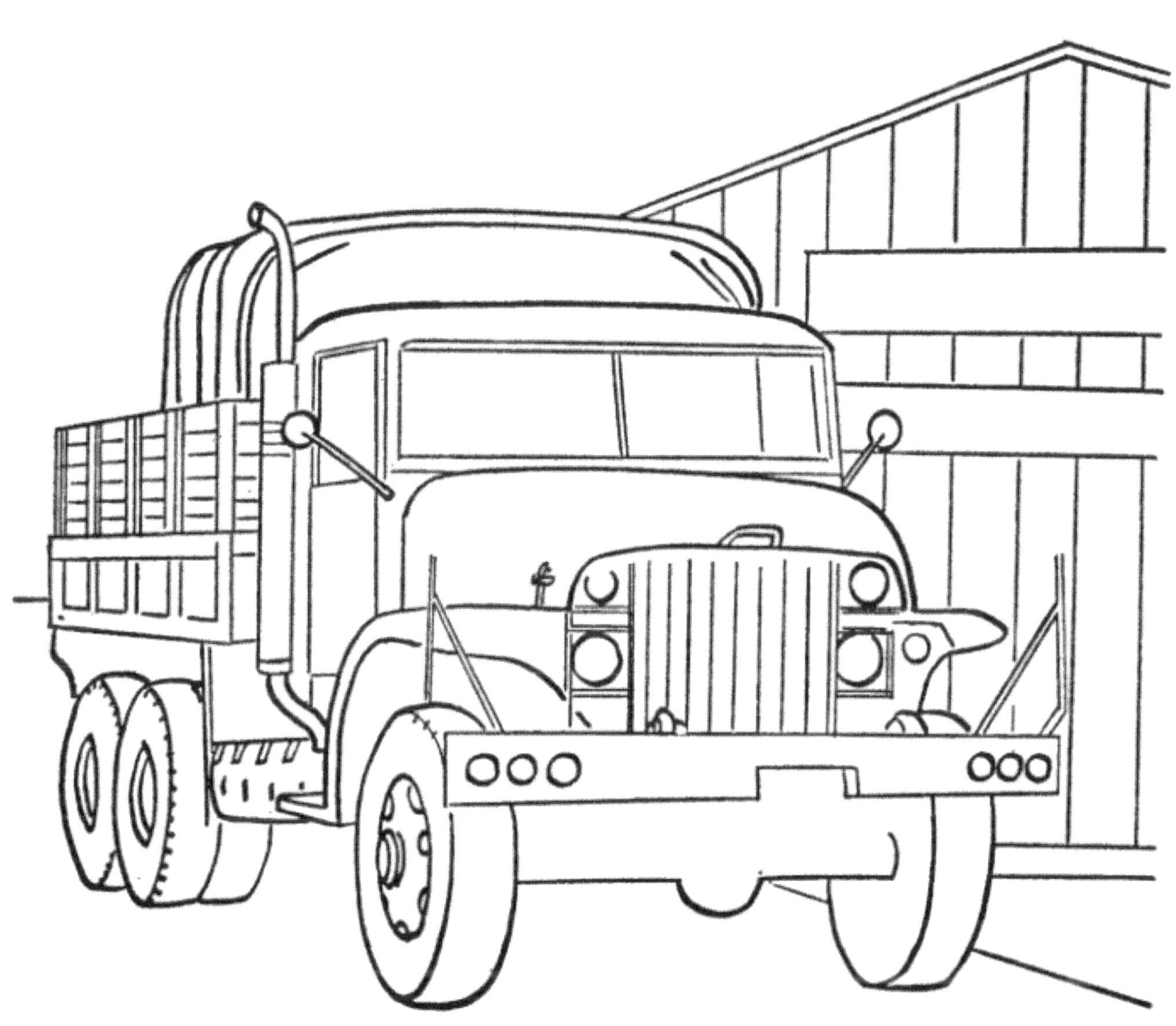

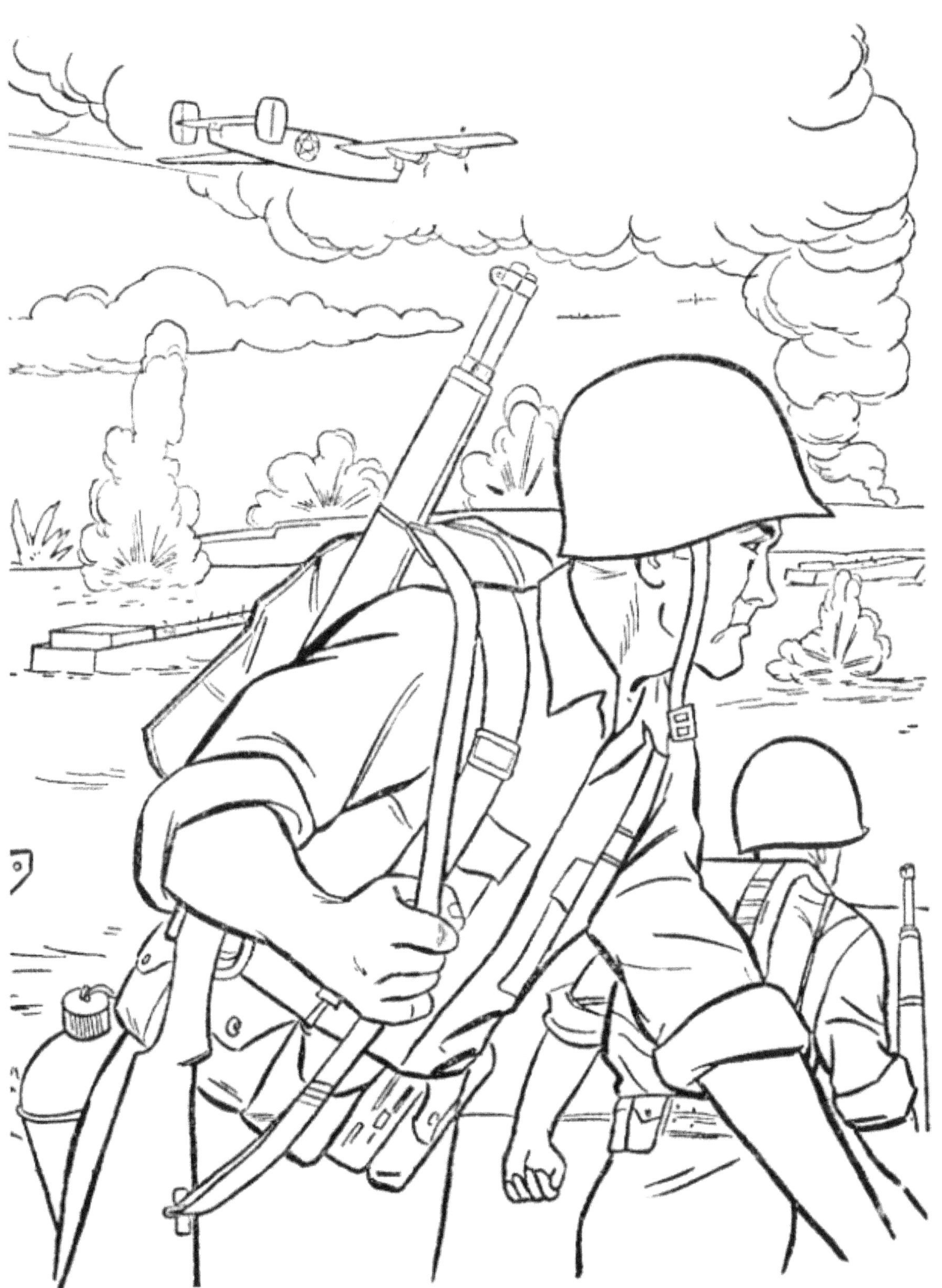

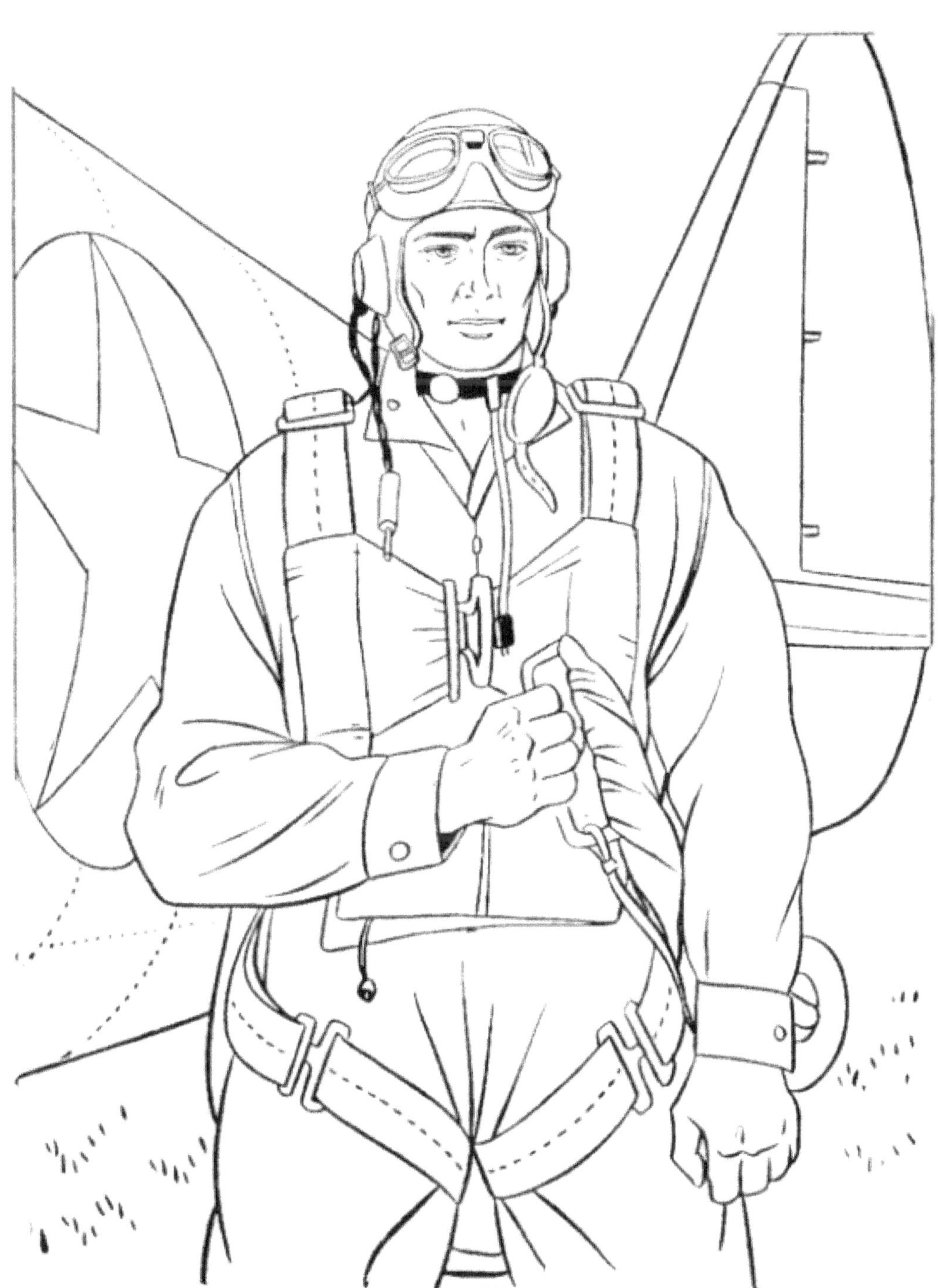

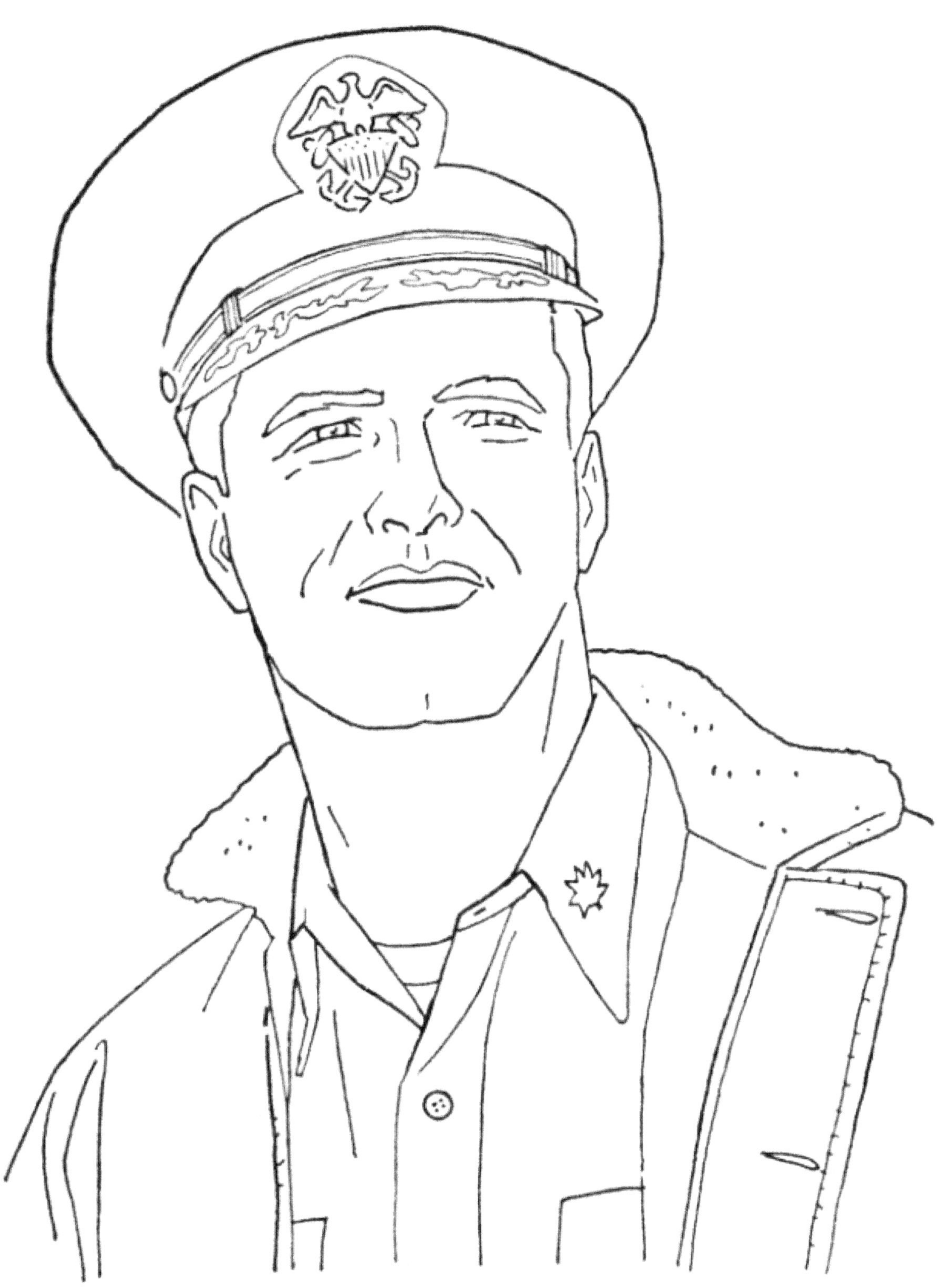

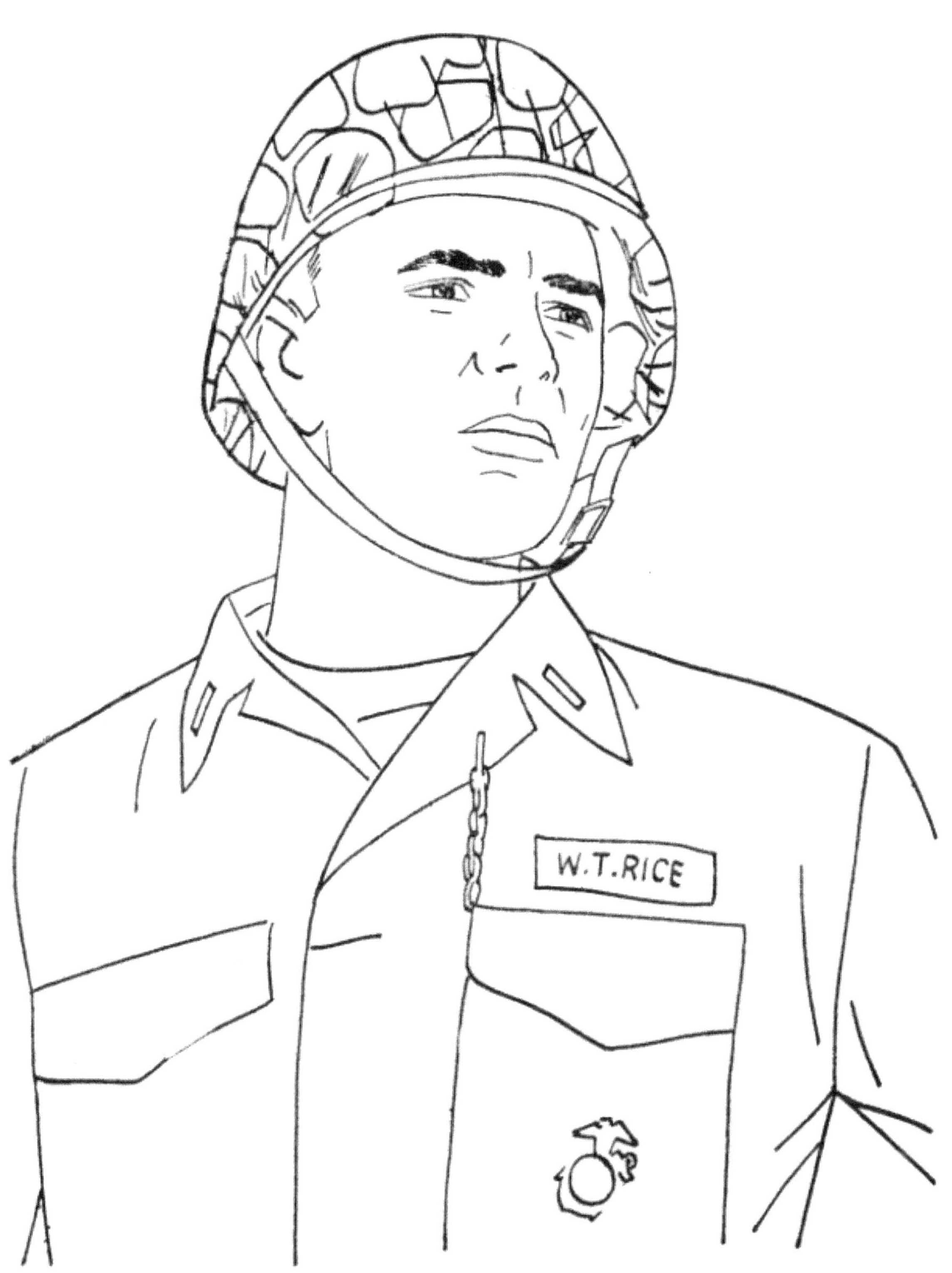

W.T.RICE

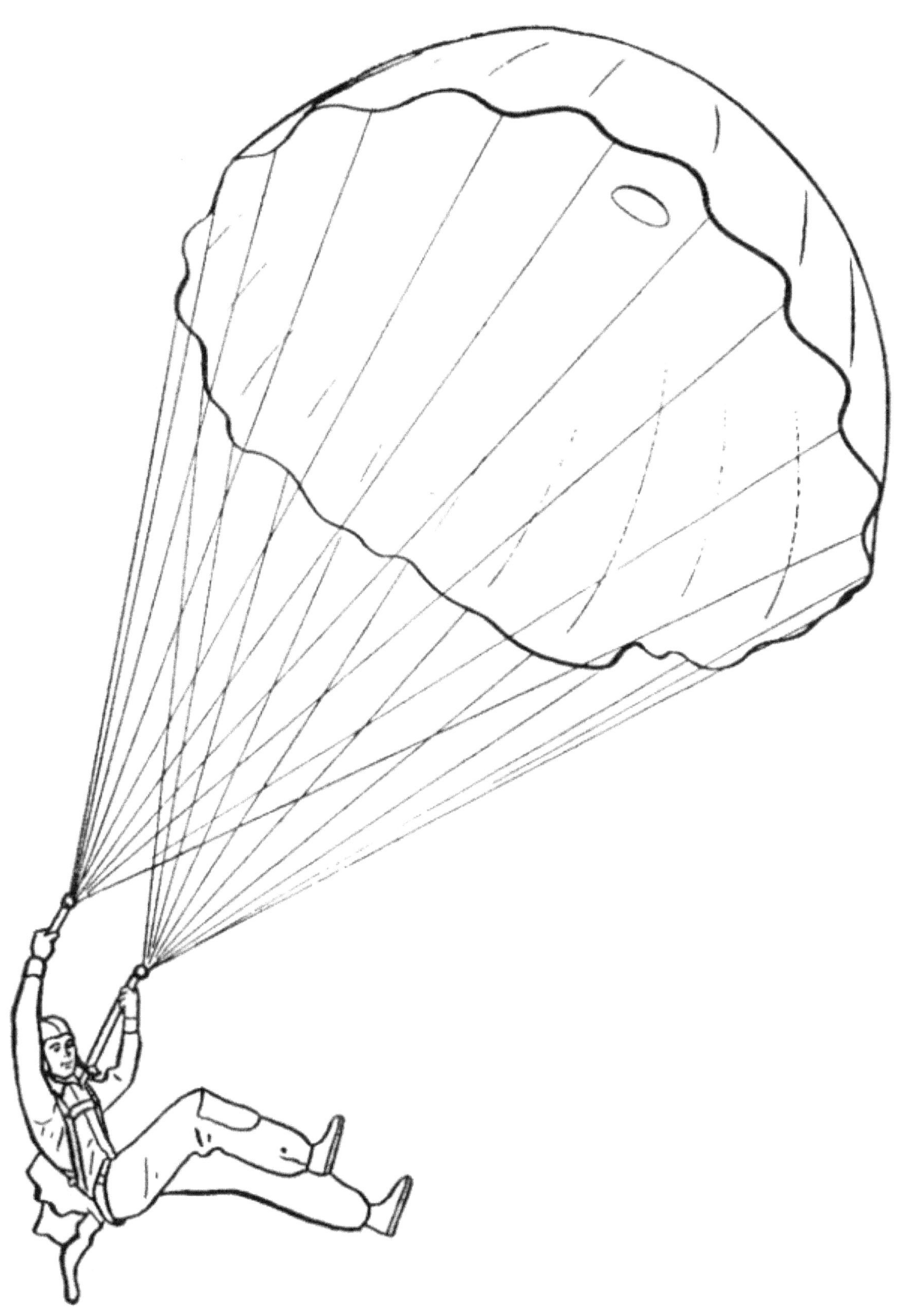

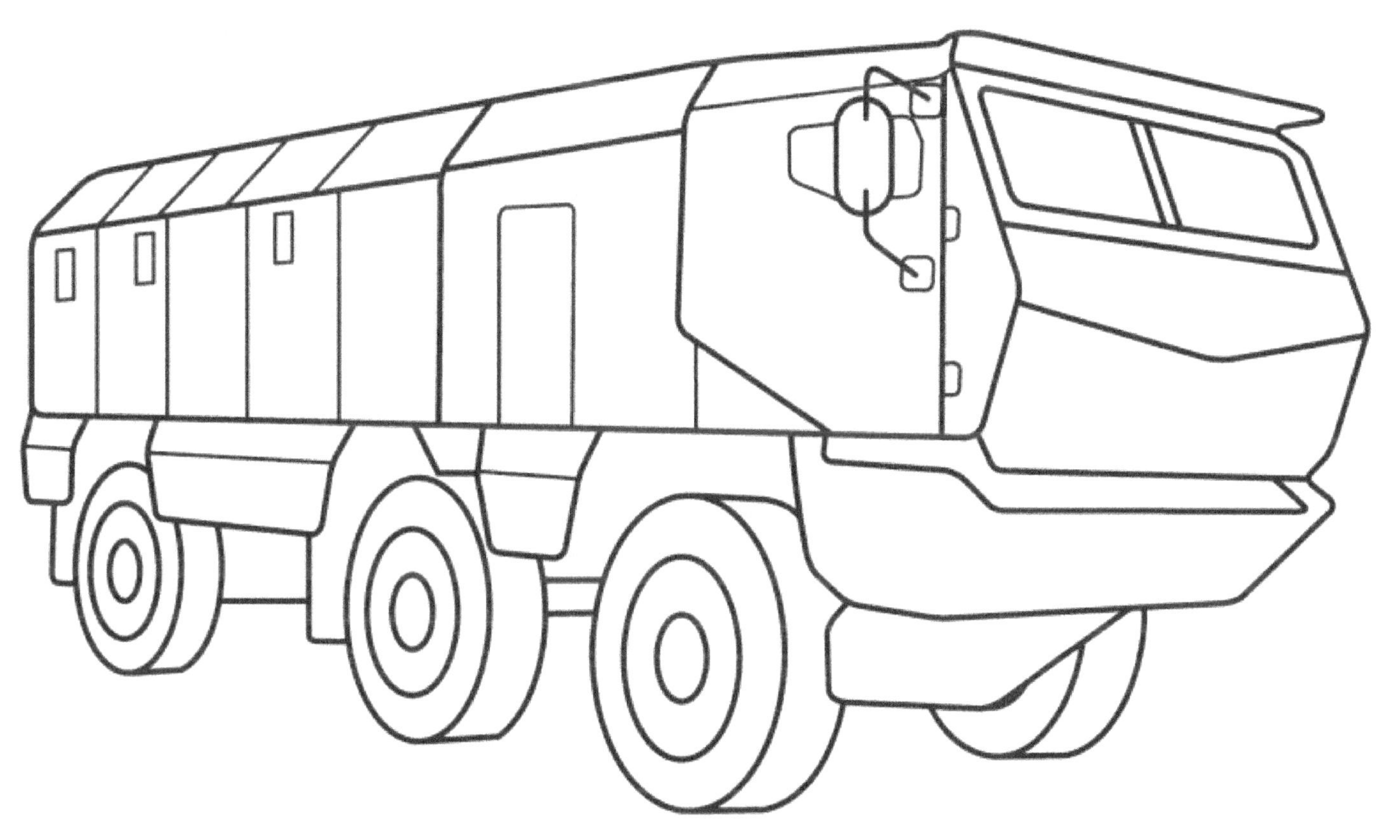

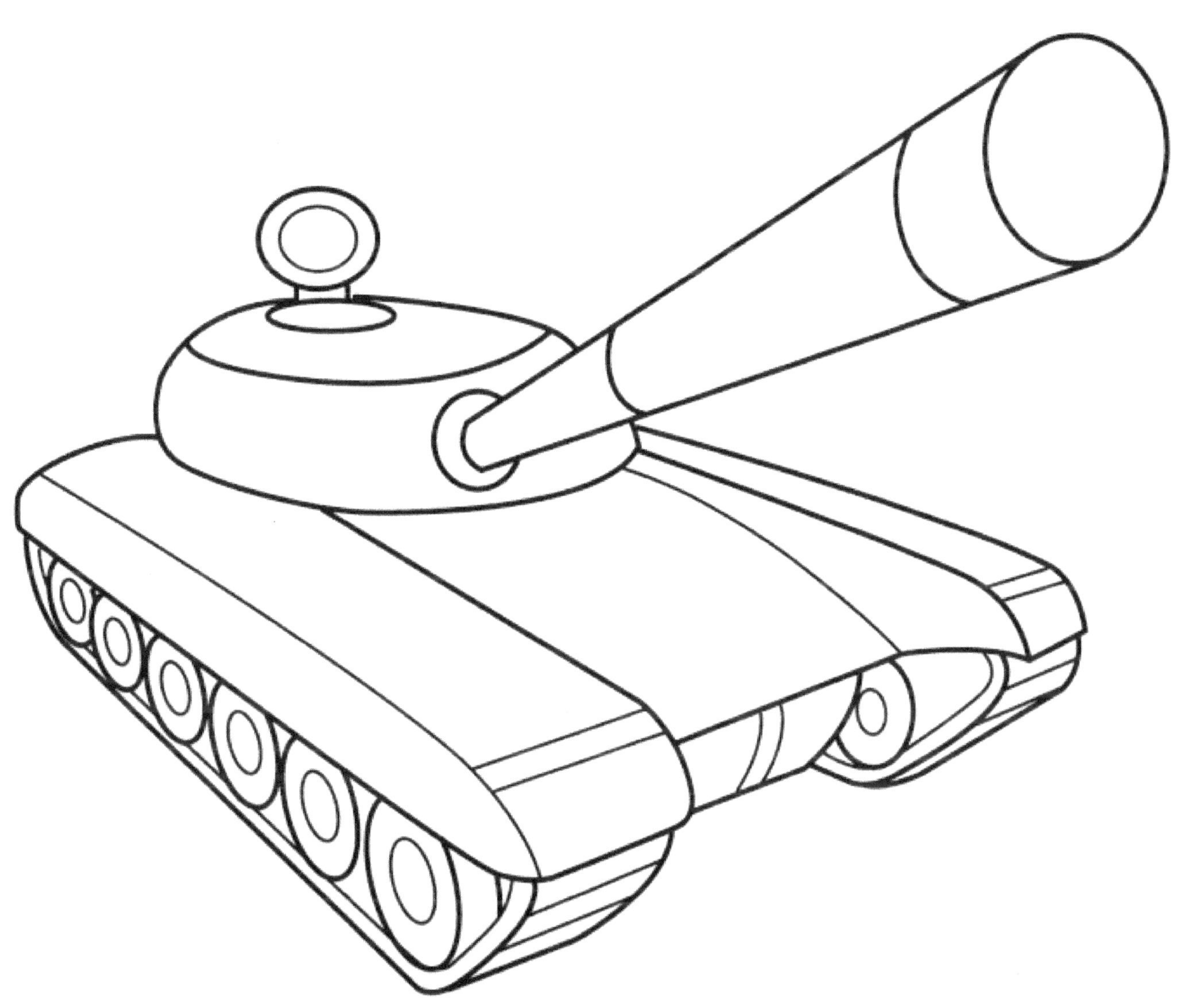

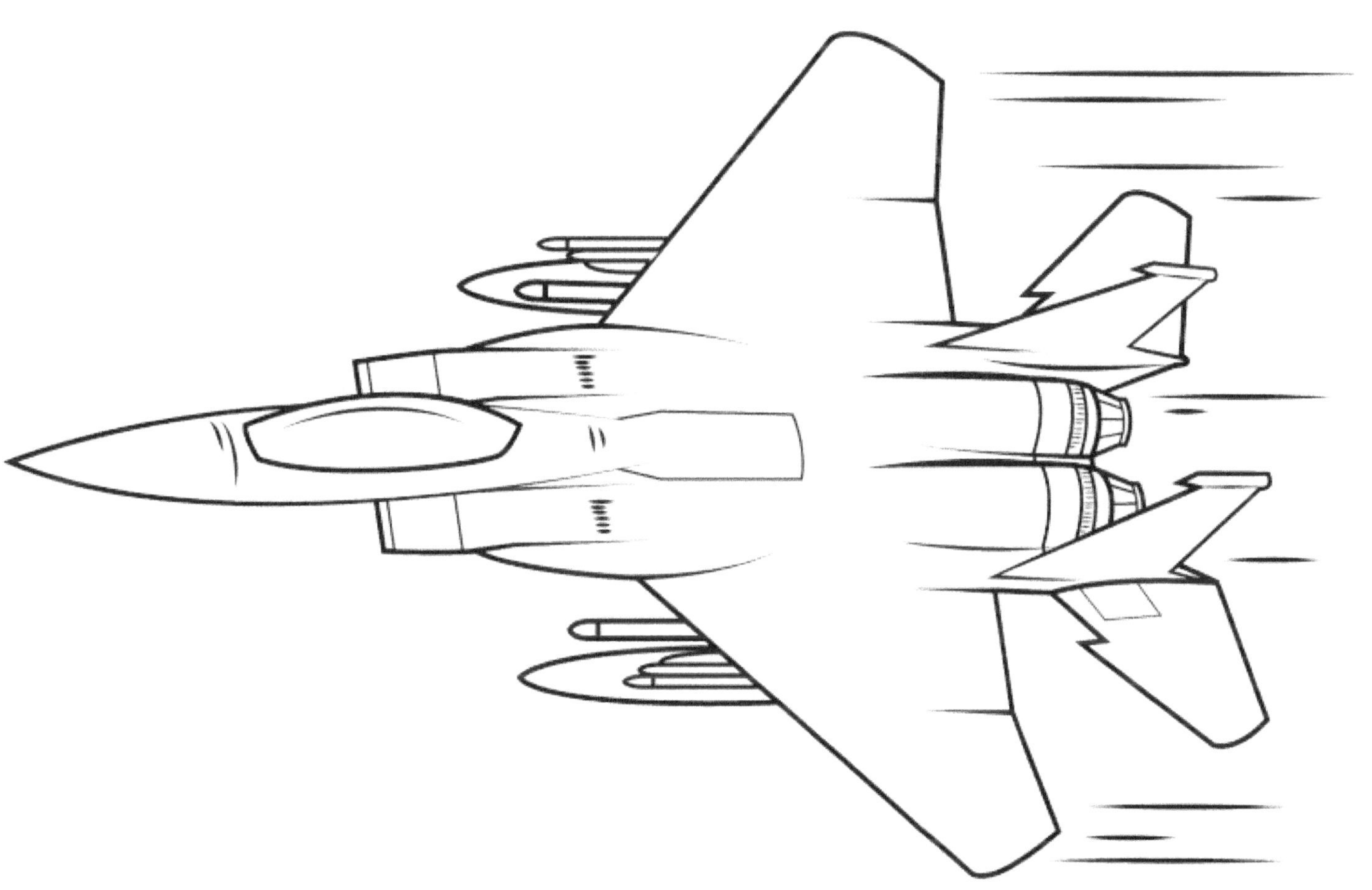

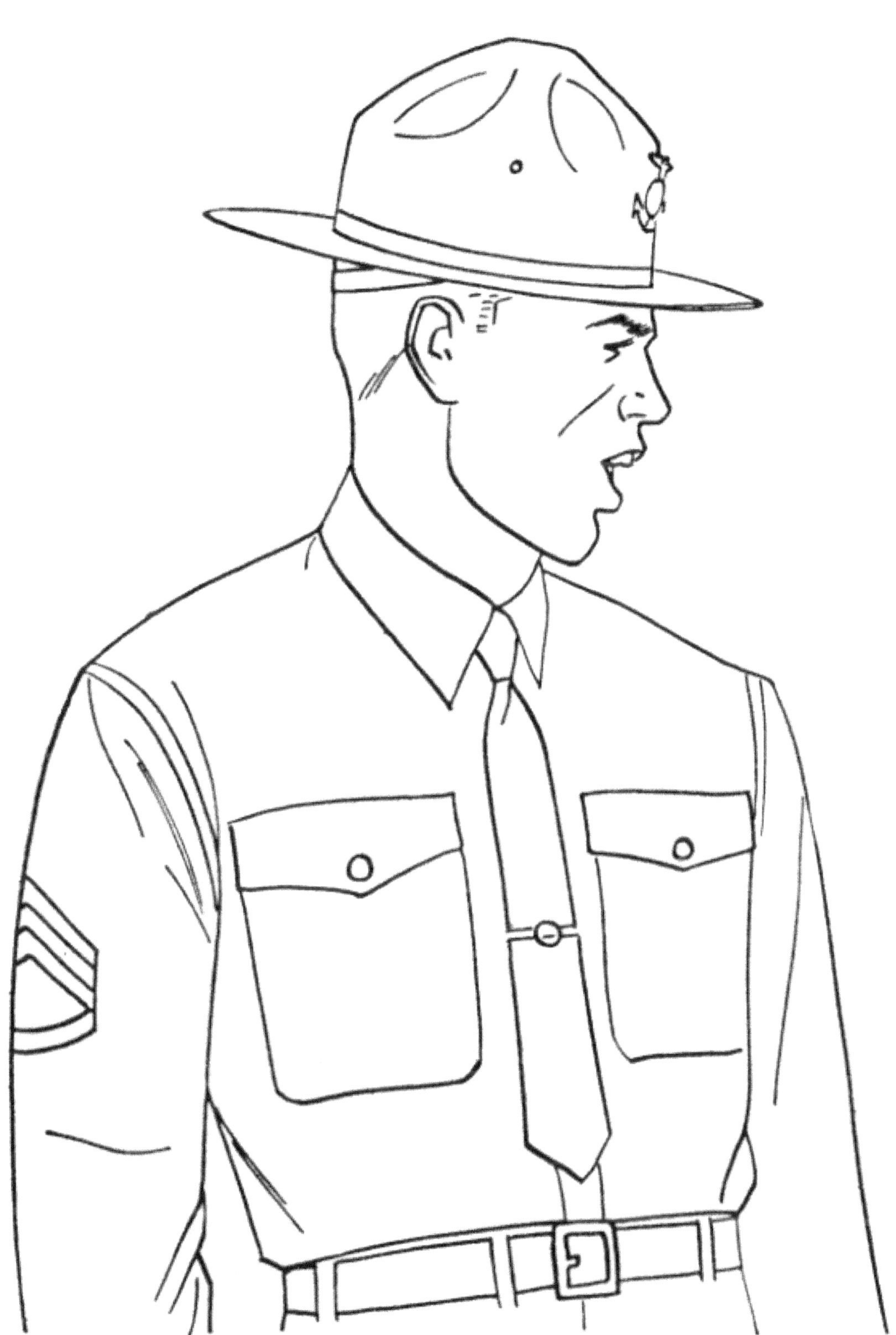

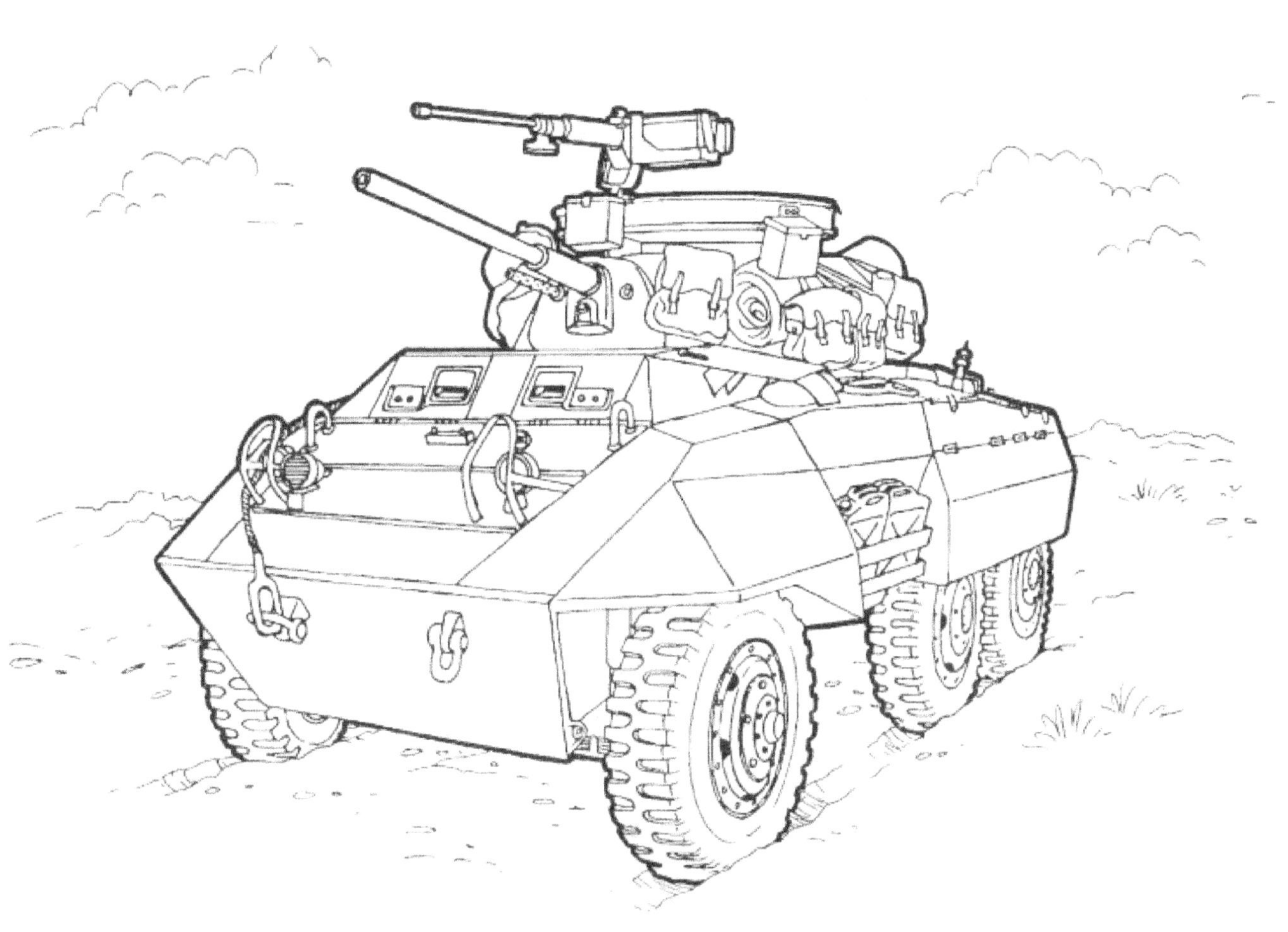

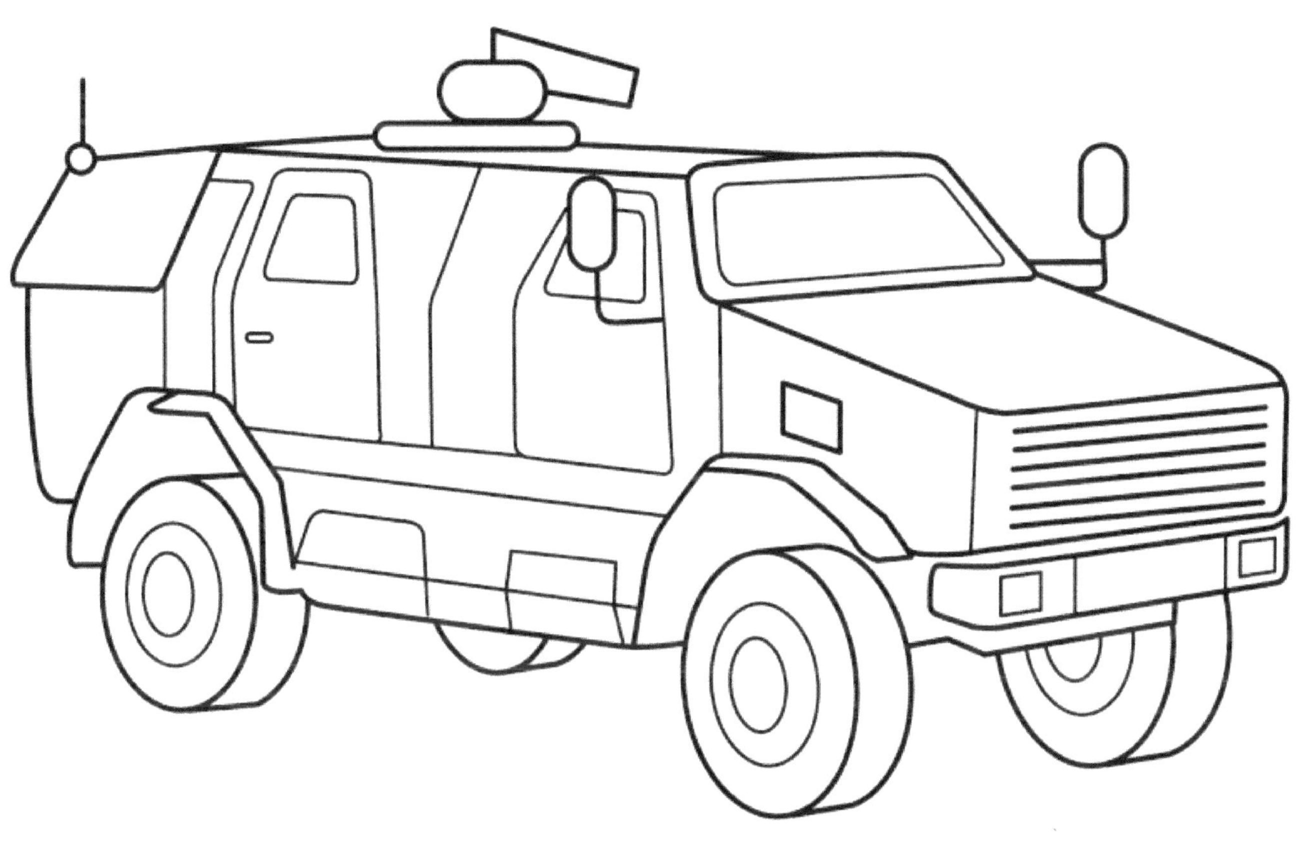

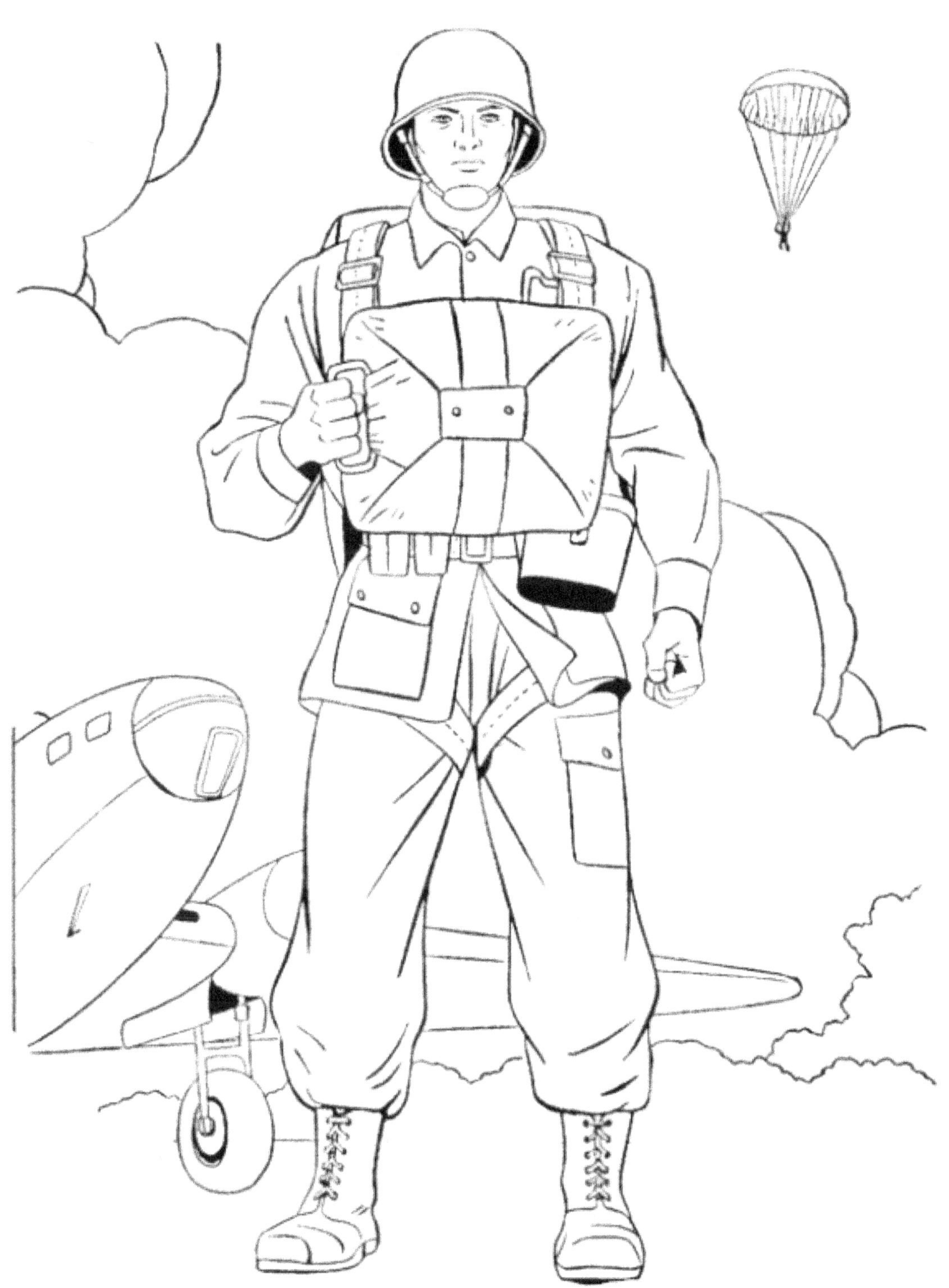

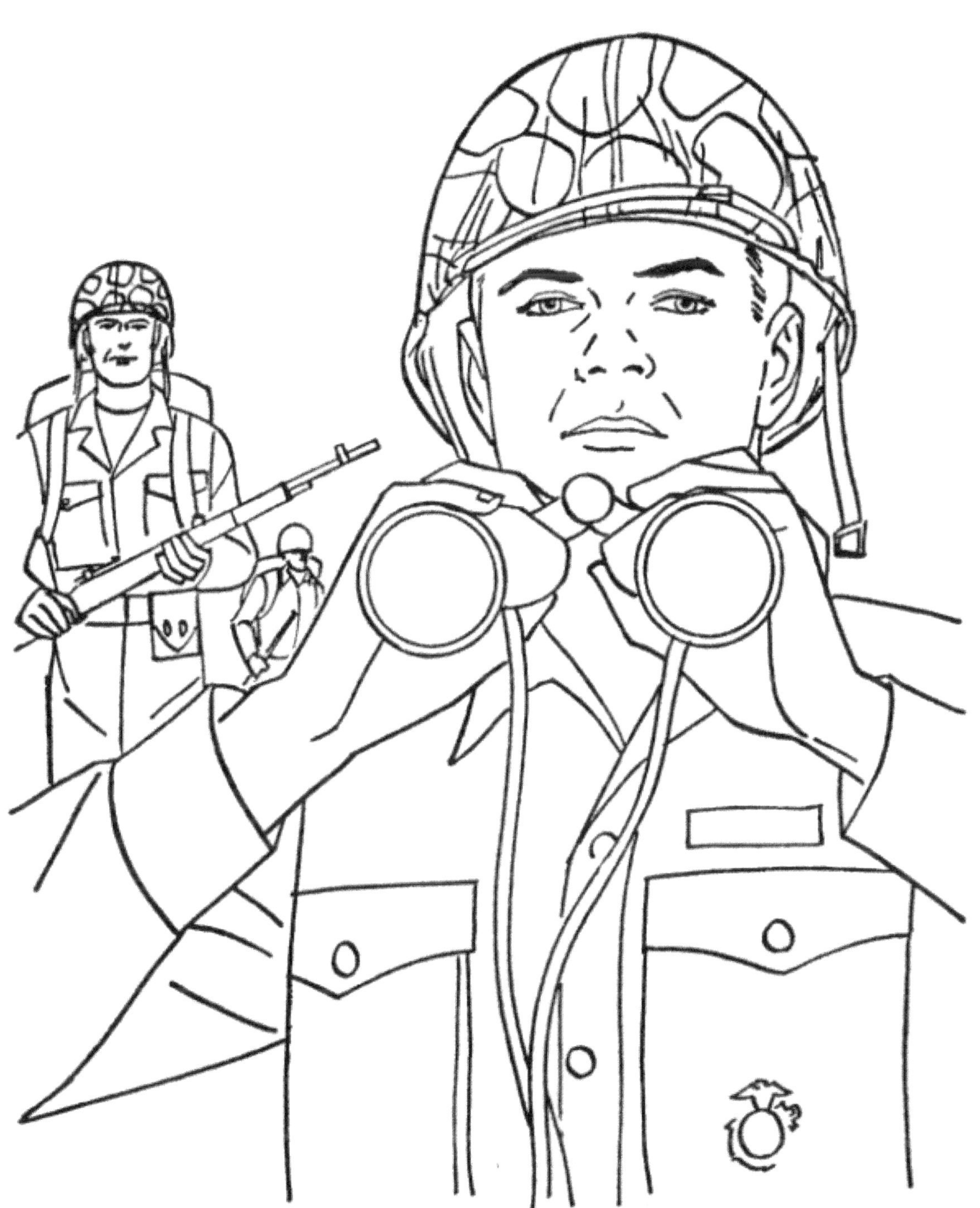